T0209660

THE STUDY
OF THE SEVEN
DISPENSATIONS

DR. GILBERT H. EDWARDS

authorHOUSE®

AuthorHouse™
1663 Liberty Drive
Bloomington, IN 47403
www.authorhouse.com
Phone: 1 (800) 839-8640

Published by AuthorHouse 05/04/2020

ISBN: 978-1-7283-6075-1 (sc)
ISBN: 978-1-7283-6076-8 (e)

Print information available on the last page.

Any people depicted in stock imagery provided by Getty Images are models,
and such images are being used for illustrative purposes only.
Certain stock imagery © Getty Images.

This book is printed on acid-free paper.

Because of the dynamic nature of the Internet, any web addresses or
links contained in this book may have changed since publication and
may no longer be valid. The views expressed in this work are solely those
of the author and do not necessarily reflect the views of the publisher,
and the publisher hereby disclaims any responsibility for them.

Scripture quotations marked KJV are from the Holy Bible, King James
Version (Authorized Version). First published in 1611. Quoted from the KJV
Classic Reference Bible, Copyright © 1983 by The Zondervan Corporation.

This book is dedicated to
The Eastern and Southern States Council
The Pentecostal Churches of the Apostolic
Faith International, Inc.
in which I was born spiritually;

and to my church family
The Full Gospel True Mission, Inc.;

and to all who read this book.

Contents

Preface

This study is to give the biblical understanding of human history from: innocence, conscience, human government, promise, law, grace and the Kingdom. Each one has a system of order or existing at a particular time. This study will point out the main characters in each dispensation; and point out their failure. Each of the dispensations end in judgement.

Introduction

In the beginning of any line of investigation, it is well to mark off as definitely as possible the field that we propose to study. This is necessary to give definiteness to our efforts; otherwise, we shall engage only in aimless wondering. Here we shall make a preliminary survey of our field and look at some phases of the subject. What is the idea and scope of human history, known as Dispensations?

Human history started on the 6th day when God created the first human. Man began as innocence until the 7th dispensation "The Kingdom." Man was tested and tried; when he failed it brought judgement. In this history of man, we see the creation of man (human), the test of obedience, the trait, fall and then the results.

Each dispensation will be discussed as well, and in each dispensation, God shows His mercy; and plans a way for salvation. This study will also point out the duration of the dispensations, the first man that was born and the first murderer. There is an intimidation in the curse imposed on Eve, "I will greatly multiply thy conception," (Genesis 3:16) that births were not only frequent, but that several children will be born at one time. There was no other way that the human race could multiply as it did in those days.

Intermarriage played a part in one of the judgements. We will look at the seven of tribulations, the Millennial and end with the White Throne Judgement.

CREATION

The seven dispensations begin with the creation of man on the 6th day (Genesis 1:1-2; 25).

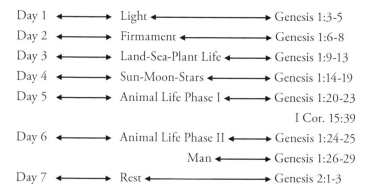

Day 1 ←——→ Light ←————————→ Genesis 1:3-5

Day 2 ←——→ Firmament ←————→ Genesis 1:6-8

Day 3 ←——→ Land-Sea-Plant Life ←——→ Genesis 1:9-13

Day 4 ←——→ Sun-Moon-Stars ←————→ Genesis 1:14-19

Day 5 ←——→ Animal Life Phase I ←——→ Genesis 1:20-23

I Cor. 15:39

Day 6 ←——→ Animal Life Phase II ←——→ Genesis 1:24-25

Man ←————→ Genesis 1:26-29

Day 7 ←——→ Rest ←————————→ Genesis 2:1-3

CHAPTER I

THE FIRST DISPENSATION – INNOCENCE

Man created, (Genesis 2:7) "And the Lord God formed a man of the dust of the ground, and breathed into his nostrils the breath of life, and man became a living soul." Man is endowed with both good inclination and an evil inclination. Man is also a citizen of two worlds; he is both of the earth and of heaven. He comes from the dust of the ground. He is a living soul. The term may mean nothing more than a "living entity", or maybe a speaking spirit (a personality) endowed with the faculty of thinking and expressing his thoughts in speech.

Genesis 1:26-28a – which was in God's future plan to reproduce the world. God started with man (Adam). The word Adam is used here in the sense of a human being (not male or female). It is derived from Adamah'-earth; to signify that man was earth-born.

In our image, after our likeness, man is made in the image and likeness of God. His character is potentially Divine. God created man to be immortal and made him to be an image of His own eternity. Man alone, among living creatures, is gifted like his Creator with moral freedom and will. He was born innocent. He is capable of knowing and loving God, and of holding spiritual communion with Him. Man alone can guide his actions in accordance with reason. On this account, he is said to have been made in the form and likeness of the Almighty. Because man is endowed with reason, he can subdue his impulses in the service of moral and religious ideals, and is born to bear rule over nature. Here is the purpose of man besides to love God:

> ". . . Be fruitful, and multiply, and replenish the earth and subdue it: and have dominion over of the fish of the sea, and over the fowl of the air, and every living thing that creepeth upon the earth." (Genesis 1:28, KJV)

<u>Be fruitful and multiply</u>. – This is the first precept given to man; the duty of building a home and rearing a family.

<u>Subdue it</u>. – The secret of all modern science is in the first chapter of the Book of Genesis. Belief in the dominion of spirit over matter, of mind over nature, of man over the physical and the animal creation, was the possession of that dominion. What we call the will or volition of man . . . has

become a power in nature, an imperium in emperor, which has profoundly modified not only man's own history, but that of the whole living world, the face of the planet on which he lives.

The Creation of Man and Woman

Genesis 1:26-28; Genesis 2:7; Genesis 2:18-25

The Commission of Man

Adam was given instructions, commands or duties. The man was told what to do, but had no knowledge of what he was purposed to do, and that is what makes him "innocent." The duty in <u>Genesis 1:28-30,</u> was what the man was to do, but he had not been in a classroom, or taught to rule, because at that time he didn't rule the Serpent, which caused Eve to eat the forbidden fruit. God instructed Adam and Eve concerning what was considered right and wrong, as you would tell your children, not to go a certain place because it is wrong, but not why it is wrong.

As a creation of God, human beings are free, but have limits. Eating from the tree of the <u>knowledge</u> of good and evil was prohibited. Human beings had no knowledge, so they disobeyed God to get knowledge. Because of their innocence, human life has been given an environment conducive to growth and entrusted with responsibility for using it well. When they ate of the forbidden fruit, their eyes were opened; the knowledge attained is neither of happiness, wisdom or power, but of sin.

The Communion of Man

Genesis 3:8-10

To communicate God's presence, the Bible often speaks of God as if He has a human form. Here in <u>Genesis 3:8-10</u>, God was present in the garden He made seeking His creatures, who had chosen to disobey His rules for living. One precept alone had they been asked to obey, and even this proved too much for them. Consciousness of sin and its conflict forfeited their innocence. They knew that they were naked – naked of all sense of gratitude and obedience to the Divine will.

The Dwelling Place of Man

Genesis 2:8-15

God placed the newly created man in a garden especially created and designed as a comfortable home for him. God created woman to be his companion, to share life with him in a complementary, mutually fulfilling relationship.

The Fall of Man

Genesis 2:17; 3:1-7

In the beginning, death has been understood as the consequence of disobedience to God. The entrance of evil and suffering unto humans was due to the sin of the man and woman. By eating of the tree's fruit in direct disobedience, the man and the woman usurped God's right to determine what is good and evil.

The Result of the Fall

Genesis 3:10-24

Man, having through disobedience, secured the faculty of unlimited knowledge. There was real danger that his knowledge would outstrip his sense of obedience to Divine Law. Through further disobedience, he could secure deathlessness. Immortality, however, that had been secured through disobedience and likened in sin, an immortal life of intellect without conscience would defeat the purpose of man's creation. Therefore, not only for his punishment but for his salvation, to bring him back from the sinister course on which he had entered, God sent man forth from the garden. Man having sunk into sin, must rise again through the spiritual purification of suffering and death. They were driven from God's presence and when man banishes God from his world, he dwells in a wilderness instead of a Garden of Eden.

Judgement of the Fall of Man

Genesis 3:1-24

"And unto Adam he said, because thou hast harkened unto the voice of thy wife, and hast eaten of the tree, of which I

> commanded thee, saying, Thou shalt not
> eat of it: cursed is the ground for thy sake;
> in sorrow shalt thou eat of it all the days of
> thy life." (Genesis 3:17, KJV)

It was Adam's duty from the beginning to till the ground (Genesis 2:15), but the work would become much more laborious. The soil would henceforth yield its produce only as a result of hard and uncasing toil. "Thou shalt eat the herb." The spontaneous growth of soil would be weeds, which are unsuitable for human beings' consumption. Man's food is the herbs, which he can only acquire by toil.

> "In the sweat of thy face shalt thou eat
> bread, till thou return unto the ground; for
> out of it wast thou taken: for dust thou art,
> and unto dust shalt thou return." (Genesis
> 3:19, KJV)

The Cursed

Genesis 3:14-19

Moral law operates in God's creation. Rebellion against God brings punishment and ultimate death. God sets limits which human beings must obey, or suffer the consequences. Creation is God's gift and retains an element of God's mystery, which humans can never know. The doctrine of creation presents a call to humans to trust God and not seek absolute freedom. Human pain, broken relationships, a non-productive environment and occupational toil are all related to human rebellion, and not to God's original intentions for human life. They represent God's gracious alternative to the expected sentence of immediate death.

> "And unto Adam he said, because thou hast harkened unto the voice of thy wife, and hast eaten of the tree, of which I commanded thee, saying, Thou shalt not eat of it: cursed is the ground for thy sake; in sorrow shalt thou eat of it all the days of thy life." (Genesis 3:17, KJV)

CHAPTER II

THE DISPENSATION OF CONSCIENCE

Judgement

2nd Dispensation – Conscience

The Flood

The Test of Conscience and Its Failure:

1. <u>Cain and Abel</u> – Genesis 4:2-11

    Where did Cain go wrong? What we give and how we give it – our attitude and purpose are both important. If you do wrong, wrong can be corrected if you listen. God saith:

    "If you do what is right . . ." God indicated to Cain what he needed to do to make his gift acceptable. Giving is a worship; God does not accept all worship acts. If we fail to please God with our worship, we have His promise that we will be accepted, if we do what is right.

As the younger brother, Abel is given the lighter task of caring for the flocks; while Cain assists his father in the cultivation of the soil. The religious instinct is part of man's nature, and sacrifice is the earliest outward expression of that worship. Its purpose was to express acknowledgment of His bounty to the Giver of all. The firstlings: the most highly prized among the flock; the fat; the richest part of the animal. God accepted Abel's offering. But Cain, unlike Abel, his sacrifice is rejected because of the difference of Spirit in which it was offered. The Lord looks to the heart. Cain was disappointed and rejected. God mercifully intervenes to arrest the progress of evil thoughts.

Sin crouches – sin is compared to a ravenous beast lying in wait for its prey. It crouches at the entrance of the house, to spring upon its victim as soon as the door is opened. By harboring feelings of vexation, Cain opened the door of his heart to the evil passions of envy, anger and violence, which eventually ended in murder. Passion and evil imaginations are ever assaulting the heart of man. Yet, he can conquer them, if only he resists them with determination. Cain took his little brother Abel far away from their parents' home, where Cain had his brother at his mercy. There Cain murdered his brother Abel. Cain became the first murder, and also he was the first man born. Not only did Cain murder his brother Abel, but he also slew Abel's unborn descendants.

2. Intermarriage – Genesis 6:1-2

It is believed in the period of ancient times, people believe that there once existed a race of men of gigantic strength and stature who were the offspring of human mother and celestial father, and this caused corruption in the land.

3. Separation: Genesis 6:4

The Judgement of Conscience

Genesis 6:6-7 (KJV) – "And it repented the Lord that he had made man on the earth, and it grieved him at his heart. And the Lord said, I will destroy man whom I have created from the face of the earth; both man, and beast, and the creeping thing, and the fowls of the air; for it repenteth me that I have made them."

Genesis 6:17 (KJV) – "And behold, I, even I, do bring a flood of waters uponthe earth, to destroy all flesh, wherein is the breath of ife, from under heavens; and everything that is in the earth shall die."

Genesis 7:4 (KJV) – "For yet seven days, and I will cause it to rain upon the earth forty days and forty nights; and every living substance that I have made will I destroy from off the face of the earth."

The Duration of Judgement

Genesis 7:11	⟶	<u>600 years, 2 months</u>	<u>17 days</u>
Genesis 8:13	⟶	<u>601 years, 1 month</u>	<u>11 days</u>
		0 years, 11 months	16 days

CHAPTER III

THE DISPENSATION OF HUMAN GOVERNMENT

Judgement

3rd Dispensation – Human Government

God's Declaration

Genesis 8:22

Babel
Genesis 11:1-9

God's Declaration – Genesis 8:22 (KJV)

"While the earth remaineth, seedtime, and harvest, and cold and heat, and summer and winter, and day and night shall not cease."

God promised those who survived the flood that the forces of nature would act with predictable harmony, people would therefore be able to plan for the future with assurance that sowing and reaping would still be a reality.

I. Instructions following the Flood

   A. Command of God – Genesis 9:1(KJV)

     "And God blessed Noah and his sons, and said unto them, Be fruitful and multiply and replenish the earth."

   B. Laws in the light of God's instruction – Genesis 9:2-4

     1. Fear – Genesis 9:2
     2. Food – Genesis 9:3
     3. Flesh – Genesis 9:4

   C. The Law of Life – Genesis 9:5-6

II. God's Promise – Genesis 9:8-17

   A. Note: Genesis 10:5, corresponds with Genesis 11:8
   B. Note: Genesis 10:10, corresponds with Genesis 11:9

III. Disobedience – Genesis 11:1-4

   A. Communication description – Genesis 11:1
   B. Place of disobedience – Genesis 11:2
   C. Act of disobedience – Genesis 11:3-4
     God created humans to have fellowship with Him and enjoy the privileges of serving their Creator. Instead, people chose to serve their

own pride and egotism. Rather than trusting God to protect them and preserve their community, they took matters into their own hands. Rebellion against God on the individual or community level is sin.

IV. Observation of God – Genesis 11:5-6

"And the Lord <u>came down</u> to see the city and the tower, which the children of men builded" (KJV) - An anthropomorphic expression: the rule that a judge should never condemn an offender without first seeing for himself both him and the nature of the offence."

V. Judgement of God – Genesis 11:7-9

(BABEL): Genesis 11:1-9

The Babel Tower was wrongness in the fact that its builders were defying the Divine command to spread abroad and replenish the earth.

"So the Lord scattered them abroad from thence upon the face of the whole earth: . . ." (KJV) - Their meaning is let's rebel!

Chapter IV

The Dispensation of Promise

4th Dispensation – Promise

Abraham's Covenant
Genesis 12:1-3
Genesis 17:6-8

Judgement

The Exodus – Exodus 1:7-14

Exodus 12 – 19:7

Abrahamic Covenant – Genesis 12:1-3; 17:6-8

". . . Get Thee out of thy country, and from thy kindred, and from thy father's house, unto a land that I will shew thee." (KJV) - In this land of idol worship - Thou art not worthy to rear sons to the service of God. The evil surroundings would contaminate them, their country – their relatives – and their father's house. These are the main influences which mold a person's thoughts and actions.

". . . I will bless Thee; and make thy name great . . ." (KJV) - at first, he will be unknown, a stranger in a strange land. ". . . And thou shalt be a blessing," (KJV) - these words contain the ideal which was set for Himself to become a blessing to humanity by the beneficial influence of his godly life and by turning others to a knowledge of God.

<u>"And I will bless them that bless thee."</u> (KJV); those who follow Abraham's teaching will, like him, enjoy God's favor.

I.   The promise of Abraham (Abram)

    A.   The Promise Land - Genesis 12:1
    B.   The Promise Nation – Genesis 12:2
    C.   The Promise Blessing – Genesis 12:3

II.   The obedience of Abraham – Genesis 12:4

In obedience to the Heavenly voice, he left the land of his birth and all the clamor and worldly prosperity of his native place. He becomes a pilgrim for life; enduring trials, famines, privations, wondering into Canaan, as a sojourner into Egypt, as a refugee and basic gain into Canaan – all for the sake of humanity, that he might share the blessing of his knowledge of God and righteousness.

III. The Abrahamic Covenant confirmed – Genesis 15:1-7

". . . Look now toward heaven, and tell the stars, if thou be able to number them; and he said unto him, so shall thy seed be." (KJV)

IV. The name changed – Genesis 17:4-5

Abraham . . . multitude of nations. Ab means "Father"; and rah am, the second half of the new name is an Arabic word for multitude. The change of his name emphasizes the mission of Abraham, which is to bring all the people under the wings of the Shechinati.

V. The Covenant eternally confirmed – Genesis 17:6-8

"And I will make thee exceeding fruitful, and I will make nations of thee, and kings shall come out of thee. And I will establish my covenant between me and thee and thy seed after thee in their generations for an everlasting covenant, to be a God unto thee and to thy seed after thee. And I will give unto thee, and to thy seed after thee, the land wherein thou art a stranger, all the land of Canaan, for an everlasting possession, and I will be their God." (KJV)

VI. God's provision as God's confirmation – Genesis 22:1-14

Abraham's faith manifested itself in obedience, illustrated by offering his son Isaac as a burnt offering in accordance with God's command. Even so, his answer to Isaac was that God would provide the Lamb for the sacrifice.

VII.   A nation named – Genesis 32:24-29

<u>No more Jacob</u>; that is the supplanter, prevailing over opponents by deceit.

<u>Israel;</u> the name is clearly a title of victory; probably a companion of God. Contenders for the Divine, conquering by strength from above.

VIII. Interference by sin – Genesis 37:20-27

"Come now therefore, and let us slay him, and cast him into some pit, and we will say, some evil beast hath devoured him; and we shall see what will become of his dreams." (KJV)

IX. Judgment – Exodus 1:7-14

   A.   Israel made slaves

      "And the Egyptians made the children of Israel to serve with rigour. And they made their lives bitter with hard bondage, in mortar and in brick, and in all manner of service in the field; in all their service, wherein they made them serve, was with rigour." (KJV)

      Serve with "rigour" – with crushing oppression, to annihilate both the emergies and the spirit of the labourer, and calculated to bring about the degeneration of the Hebrew race.

B. Redemption by blood – Exodus 12:12-13; 12:29

"And the blood shall be to you for a token upon the houses where ye are; and when I see the blood, I will pass over you, and the plague shall not be upon you to destroy you, when I smite the land of Egypt." (KJV)

I will pass over you. – I will spare you; I will protect you. No plague be upon you – the angel of destruction will not have permission to bring the plague upon you.

C. Israel leaves Egypt – Exodus 12:30-43

"It was a night to be much observed unto the Lord for bringing them out of the land of Egypt; this is that night of the Lord to be observed of all the children of Israel in their generations." (KJV)

Of watching – Of keeping in mind, of celebration, and of vigilance; because God shields them, and did not suffer destruction to approach their houses. He ordered that the night be observed by all Israelites as a night of watching, a memorial of the night of redemption. It was the birthright of the Israelite nation, and the whole history of Israel is stamped with its memory.

Chapter V

The Dispensation of Law

5th Law · Exodus 19:8 · Judgement · Matthew 27:50

I. Begins with submission – Exodus 19:8

> "And all the people answered together, and said; "all that the Lord hath spoken we will do. . ." (KJV)

Moses came from the Mount to the Elders, who reported to the people. Giving the entire nation the choice of accepting or rejecting the Divine message. The people gladly and freely expressed their willingness to inter God's covenant; Exodus 24:3. They thereby become in a special sense God's people.

Moses returned to the mountain and God knew their reply. He immediately declared His intention of revealing Himself in the hearing of the people.

II. Communication – Exodus 19:9-25

"And the Lord said unto Moses; "Lo, I come unto thee in a thick cloud (the difference in communication in Adam's time, which God spoke to Adam directly in the cool of the day.), that the people may hear when I speak with thee, and believer thee, forever. . . ." (KJV)

<u>That the people may hear</u> – directly and not through a messenger or an intermediary (20:16)

<u>also believer Thee</u> – the pronoun "Thee" is emphatic. Having heard the voice from the cloud and fire, the people would nevermore doubt the Divine mission of Moses. From now on, the people knew that Moses had direct communication with God and that his words were not creations of his own mind.

<u>For ever</u> – the Law of Moses will not be changed, and there will never be any other Torah from the Creator, blessed be His name.

III. <u>The Basic Law – Exodus 20:1-17.</u>

The ten words or commandments, the Decalogue are supreme among the precepts of the Torah, both on account of their fundamental and far-reaching importance and an account of the awe-inspiring manner in which they were revealed to the whole nation. Amid thunder and lightning, and the Shofar, amid flames of fire that enveloped the smoking mountain, a majestic voice pronounced that words which from that day to this have been the guide of conduct to mankind that revelation was the most remarkable event in the history of humanity. It was the birth hour of the religion of the Spirit, which was destine in time to illumine the soul, and order the live of all the children of men.

The First Table: Duties toward God.

The Second Table: Duties towards fellow-men.

IV. The Expanded Law – Exodus 20:18-23:13
This section is a body of miscellaneous laws – Civil, Criminal, Moral and Religious

The Book of the Covenant
(Exodus 20:19-23:33)

Exodus 20:19-23 – How God is to be worshipped.

19. Ye yourselves have seen; you have been eye witnesses; and know the reality of my revelation.

From heaven; in an overwhelming and incomparable manner.

20 <u>make with me – gods</u>; The regulations concerning worship begin by repeating the prohibition of idol worship, even if the idol be of silver or gold.

21 <u>an altar of earth</u>; not even an altar of stone is essential for worshipping God.

22 an altar of stone; is permissible, but the stones must be of unhewn natural rock, with the stamp of God's handiwork alone.

23 <u>uncovered</u>; "Lest the clothes of the priest be disturbed and his limbs uncovered.

V. The Law for the Order of Worship (Exodus 24:1-31:18)

> "And He said unto Moses, come up unto the Lord, thou, and Aaron, Nadab and Abihu, and seventy of the elders of Israel; and worship ye afar off." (KJV)

Moses alone was summoned to penetrate within the cloud and remained there forty days.

<u>come up</u>; this command was addressed to Moses when he was about to descend; and we are to supply before these words, place my Laws before the people and then.

<u>worship ye</u>; prepare yourselves for the Divine vision which you are about to behold.

> "And thou shalt take the atonement money of the children of Israel, and shalt appoint it for the service of the tabernacle of the congregation; that it may be a memorial unto the children of Israel before the Lord, to make an atonement for your souls." (Exodus 30:16) (KJV)

<u>a memorial</u>; that the Lord remember the children of Israel in grace, and grant them atonement for blood, shed in battle.

<u>in later ages;</u> the half-shekel became an annual tax devoted to maintaining the public services of the temple; the daily worship was carried on by the entire people and not by the gifts of a few rich donors.

VI. The Proclamation of the People's Final Rejection - Matthew 27:15-26

All efforts of unrighteousness magistrates to screen themselves from guilt in knowingly condemning the innocent or acquitting the guilty, will be fruitless. They may deceive themselves and their fellow men, but they cannot deceive God. He will hold them responsible, and the measures they take to hide their guilt will only increase their wickedness and aggravate their condemnation. It is a fearful thing to incur the guilt of blood. When un-righteously shed, it rises to heaven for vengeance. The state of the Jews for eighteen hundred years shows that the guilt of shedding the blood of Jesus Christ was lawful, and that God is just.

VII. The Calvary Judgement – Matthew 27:35-66

    A. The Cross, the Act; Matthew 27:35-50

> Refusing to take a pain killer, Jesus faced death full conscious of His pain and of the actions around Him.

>> "And they crucified Him, and parted His garments, casting lots: that it might be fulfilled which was spoken by the prophet, they parted my garments among them, and upon my vesture did they cast lots." (Matthew 27:35) (KJV)

The seven last sayings of Jesus Christ on the cross:

    (1) Supplication: "Father, forgive them, for they do not know what they are doing." (Luke 23:34)

    (2) Salvation: "I tell you the truth, today you will be with me in paradise." (Luke 23:43)

(3) Solicitation: to His mother, "Dear woman, here is your son.", and to His disciple, "Here is your mother." (John 19:36)

(4) Separation: "Eloi, Eloi, Lanasabachthani" - which means, "My God, My God, why have you forsaken me?" (Matthew 27:46)

(5) Sensation: "I am thirsty." (John 19:28)

(6) Satisfaction: "It is finished." (John 19:30)

(7) Summation: "Father, into your hands I commit my Spirit." (Luke 23:46)

The events on the cross between nine o'clock until noon defy human comprehension. For three hours, the sky gave forth no light, as Jesus took all the sins of the whole world on His body. (I Corinthians 5:21; Isaiah 53:1-12) He yielded up the ghost, He gave up His life.

B. God's Proclamation – Matthew 27:51-54

"And, behold, the veil of the temple was rent in twain from the top to the bottom; and the earth did quake, and the rocks rent; and the graves were opened; and many bodies of the saints which slept arose, and came out of the graves after His resurrection, and went into the holy city, and appeared unto many." (KJV)

At the precise moment when Jesus finished His work on the cross, the veil in the temple was torn in two by the hand of God, from top to bottom. There was no further need for this structure. Its purpose for existence had been fulfilled. The symbols it offered were not fully realized in Jesus Christ's substitutionary and atoning death. It was only a shadow of things to come; in Jesus the substance was revealed. The veil in the temple separated the people from God. Only the High Priest was permitted entrance into this holy chamber. Once there, the High Priest would sprinkle sacrificial blood upon the mercy seat as a symbol of God's presence with the supreme substitutionary sacrifice of Himself. The sign of God's approval with this sacrifice is displayed in the severed curtain. No longer would there be any need for a High Priest or animal sacrifice; for in Jesus every symbol of the temple has been fulfilled.

Veil of the temple; which separated the most holy place from the other parts of the temple. By this was signified that now the way into God's

(1) God's work – Matthew 27:51-53

(2) Man's acknowledgment – Matthew 27:54

C. Man's final attempt to do away with God –
    Matthew 27:62-66

"Now the next day, that followed the day of the preparation, the Chief Priests and Pharisees came together unto Pilate, saying Sir, we remember that that deceiver said, while He was yet alive, after three days I will rise again. Command therefore that the sepulcher be made sure until the third day, lest His disciples come by night, and steal Him away, and say unto the people, He is risen from the dead: So the last error shall be worst than the first. Pilot said unto them, ye have a watch; go your way, make it as sure as you can. So they went, and made the sepulcher sure, sealing the stone, and setting a watch." (KJV)

The next day: the first day of the week-long Passover Feast was called preparation Day because everything was made ready on that day for the remainder of the week. This would have been Friday, (We call it Good Friday.) and the next day would be Saturday, but it must be remembered that on this day, according to Jewish reckoning, began immediately after sunset on Friday evening. The activities being discussed here then, occurred just moments after Jesus' crucifixion and burial.

<u>Go make the tomb secure</u>; the religious leaders were a determined lot. They would see their job through to the very end. They were afraid of the rumors regarding Jesus' resurrection, and they feared that Jesus' disciples might plot some hoax resurrection by stealing Jesus' body from the tomb. So, they sought the militia to guard the tomb from any attempted theft of the corpse. These added measures of precaution only served to further validate the reality of Jesus' miraculous resurrection. The role of Satan in all of this activity is plainly evident. He hated Jesus from the start. He wanted to see him killed and now he wanted to see to it that he stayed dead. But God always has a way of using Satan against his own evil purposes.

Jesus' death had been a part of God's blueprints all along. His resurrection had been likewise, and Satan would not be able to stop it from happening. The greatest of all the miracles could not be prevented. Jesus would have to rise from the dead, and God would see that it would happen. Men cannot by any efforts thwart the purposes of God. "A man's heart deviseth his way; but the Lord directeth his steps." (Proverbs 16:9 KJV) "There are many devices in a man's heart; nevertheless, the counsel of the Lord, that shall stand." (Proverbs 19:21 KJV)

All the efforts of the Jews to show that Jesus Christ was guilty, only tended more clearly to show, and more striking to illustrate, his innocence and their own guilt. All of their efforts after He was dead to prevent His resurrection only tended more clearly to demonstrate that He had risen.

Chapter VI

The Dispensation of Grace

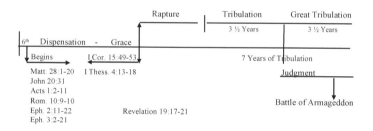

I. Age of Grace Begins

A. Key to beginning of the age of Grace – Matthew 28:1-20

(1) Resurrection of Jesus Christ – Matthew 28:1-10

"In the end of the Sabbath, as it began to dawn toward the first day of the week, came Mary

Magdalene and the other Mary to see the sepulchre." (KJV)

Jesus arose on the first day of the week – Sunday. Elsewhere this is called "The Lord's Day" (Revelation 1:10). In the days before Christ's resurrection, believers assembled in the synagogue on Saturday – the Sabbath – for worship. But now they would meet on a new day – the Lord's Day – in order to commemorate Christ's resurrection from the dead, as well as their own resurrection out of sin and eternal judgement (Acts 20:7; I Corinthians 16:1-2; C2:16-17).

"And, behold, there was a great earthquake: for an angel of the Lord descended from heaven, and came and rolled back the stone from the door, and sat upon it. His countenance was like lightening and his raiment white as snow: and for fear of Him the keepers did shake, and became as dead men. And the angel answered and said unto the woman, fear not ye; for I know that ye seek Jesus, which was crucified. He is not here; for he is risen, as he said. Come, see the place where the

Lord lay. And go quickly, and tell his disciples; that he is risen from the dead; and, behold, he goeth before you into Galilee; there shall ye see him, Lo, I have told you." (KJV)

On this day, several women journeyed to the tomb where Joseph had laid Jesus' body. They were not slightly shocked to be addressed by an angel and to see the empty grave. But their ears were coupled with joy as they heard the angelic messenger announce he is risen. This is a tremendous scene. The women had come to a grave site, but it was not the end of things, as they might suspect; instead it is just the beginning. The work has only begun. It is time to turn the hearts of Jesus' followers from bitter disappointment to utter ecstacy. The good news could not be better than what they hear today, He is risen! He is risen!

(2) The attempted cover-up – Matthew 28:11-20

The resurrection plot: the soldiers who guarded the grave site must have been terribly afraid when the dazzling white angel appeared before them. First their eyes were stunned; then their feet trembled as an earthquake shook the ground; and finally, their ears vibrated as they heard the seal being broken and the stone being rolled away! Immediately, they ran to the Chief Priest to tell him what startling thing had taken place. The leaders were perplexed, to say the least. What should they do? They decided to call the elder religious leaders for opinions. Finally, they made a decision – they would pay the soldiers to lie, and that's precisely what they did.

"Now when they were going, behold, some of the watch came into the city, and shewed unto the Chief Priest all the things that were done. And when they were assembled with the elders, and had taken counsel, they gave large money unto the soldiers, saying, say ye, his disciples came by night, and stole him away while we slept. And if this come to the Governor's ears, we will persuade him, and secure you, so they took the money, and did as they were taught: and this saying is commonly reported among the Jews until this day." (KJV)

So the soldiers took the money and did as they were instructed. All the scheming and bribing could not conceal this truth. It could not be hidden or dismissed. It was destined to be heard. The reality of

Jesus Christ's resurrection has marched triumphantly through the centuries, and found a joyful response in each generation. Christ had won!

The grave could not hold Him! Men and demons could not defeat Him, even after they had killed Him! He would rise, and His victory would transform millions, because the good news of the glorified Savior could not be stopped. Not even by a tombstone!

(3) The appearing and instructions of Jesus Christ – Matthew 28:16-20

> "Then the eleven disciples went away into Galilee, into a mountain where Jesus had appointed them. And when they say him, they worshipped him; but some doubted. And Jesus came and spake unto them, saying, all power is given unto me in heaven and in earth." (KJV)

The Great Commission is for more than a charge to make converts or to erect a church building. It is instead, both a challenge and a command to win people to Jesus Christ, and then to transform them into mature disciples, who will joyfully and consistently walk a straight line with regard to God's will. This is the Great Commission/nothing more, nothing less, and nothing less.

Once Jesus was crucified, the disciples were crushed. No pain, sorrow or grief could match their desolation. Added to their trauma was the vexing mental torment of being terribly confused. Their dreams had been shattered. Their hopes had been turned to despair, and doubt was replacing faith in the life of some disciples. Then, just as dramatically as He had disappeared, Jesus suddenly appeared again with His disciples. The experience was almost too much for them to comprehend. Then Jesus began to teach them, His topic was "Authority." Jesus wanted them to know that now He was the Commander-in-Chief of the Universe. No one – in either heaven or earth – holds a higher position of authority. Nothing is outside of His immediate control. Satan cannot act without His approval. Governments, (including the Sanhedrin) cannot make a single decision without His permission. There is not a single event that can occur apart from His direct consent. All authority now belongs to Him.

"Go ye therefore, and teach all nations,

baptizing them in the name of the Father, and of the Son, and of the Holy Ghost. Teaching them to observe all things whatsoever I have commanded you: and, lo, I am with you alway, even unto the end of the world." (KJV)

B. The purpose of the written word in the age of Grace – John 20:31

> "But these are written, that ye might believe that Jesus is the Christ, the Son of God; and that believing ye might have life through his name." (KJV)

As the object of God in causing His truth to be written and printed was, that men might believe and be saved. All should be taught, and should be disposed to read it. It was given in this form to promote the salvation of men, and is often rendered effectual by the Holy Spirit for this purpose. It should therefore, without hindrance and without delay, be circulated among all people.

C. Information by Christ and Ascension of Christ – Acts 1:2-11

(1) Information given – Acts 1:2-9

Luke wrote two books to Theophilus (Luke 1:3). The first centered on Jesus Christ's acts and teachings. The second (Acts) centered on the work of the Holy Spirit through the Apostles to spread the gospel throughout the world of the Roman Empire. Under the Spirit's power, the Apostles' preaching continued through Christ's Revelation.

"The former treatise have I made, O Theophilus, of all that Jesus began both to do and teach." (Acts 1:1 KJV)

The former treatise; the Gospel of Luke. The Book of Acts was written by Luke, and addressed to the same individual to whom he addressed his gospel. Luke 1:3 – began both to do and teach; the meaning is that he has given Jesus' works and teachings from the beginning.

(2) Ascension – Acts 1:10-11

"And while they looked steadfastly towards heaven as he went up, behold, two men stood by them in white

> apparel; which also said, ye
> men of Galilee, why stand ye
> gazing up into heaven? This
> same Jesus, which is taken up
> from you into heaven, shall
> so come in like manner, as ye
> have seen him go into heaven."
> (KJV)

Luke, in Acts, gives the fullest expression of Jesus' ascension. The ascension in Acts is coupled with the mission mandate of Church and promise of spiritual power and presence (v.8). The earthly existence of Jesus ended with a note of promise about His ultimate coming and His eternal ministry.

D.   Salvation in the Age of Grace – Romans 10:9-10; Ephesians 2:8-9

> "That if thou shalt confess with thy
> mouth the Lord Jesus, and shalt
> believe in thine heart that God
> hath raised him from the dead,
> thou shalt be saved." (KJV)

Confession and belief belong together like a hand and glove. Those who confess Jesus as Lord will be saved. A believer will confess Jesus Christ publicly. Believing and confessing are not two stages in a process, but two parts of one action.

E. The position of the Church – Ephesians 2:11-22

The Church is a reconciled community. Reconciliation is part of Jesus Christ's work. He brings all people unto Himself. Jews possessed the promises of God through the covenants, but in Jewish understanding, Gentiles possessed nothing to bring them to God. Through Jesus Christ's death, God brought both Jew and Gentile unto Him, fulfilling His promise to Abraham. (Genesis 12:1-3)

The Church has no basis for excluding any groups of people. The Church is called to invite all persons to follow Jesus Christ in faith.

F. The Church a Mystery – Ephesians 3:1-21

The mystery; namely that explained in verse 6, that the Gentiles through faith in Jesus Christ, were to be partakers of His salvation on equal terms with the Jews, and without the observance of Jewish ceremonies.

What is fellowship of the mystery? The mystery is that, through faith in Jesus Christ, Gentiles and Jews were to be reunited to God and one another in holy fellowship and communion forever. The fellowship of the mystery would be the fellowship of Gentiles with Jews, which the revelation of this mystery discloses, but another and better authenticated reading is.

What is dispensation of the mystery? That is, a dispensation which has the revelation of this mystery, as its foundation principle. <u>Hid in God</u>; hid, as it were among the secret counsel of God; who created all things according to His own counsel. <u>By the Church</u>; by means of God dealing with the Church.

II. The Rapture

    A. The First Corinthian Account – I Corinthians 15:49-53

    Flesh and blood cannot inherit; our bodies must undergo a change, such as effected in the resurrection, in order to fit them to live in heaven. Not all sleep; Christians who shall be living at the end of the world will not die, but will experience a change similar to that which those who have dies experience in the resurrection, that they may be spiritual, incorruptible and immortal.

    B. First Thessalonian Account – I Thessalonian 4:13-18

    Asleep; asleep in Jesus, who have died in union with Christ by faith, others; the unenlightened heathen; who have no hope of a resurrection and like of blessedness, with Christ in heaven. <u>Will bring with Him</u>; raised from the dead in glorious, immoral bodies, so that they, as well as those that remain alive at Jesus Christ's coming, shall appear with Him in glory. (I Corinthians 15:51-54) <u>Which are alive</u>; when the Lord shall come to judgement. <u>Shall not prevent</u>; no go before, or rise to meet the Lord before those do who are dead. <u>Rise first</u>; before the living shall be changed, and both ascend together to be forever with the Lord.

C. How we know the Rapture precedes the Tribulation.

(1) The Church is saved from the wrath of God. –

I Thessalonian 5:9-10

"For God hath not appointed us to wrath, but to obtain salvation by our Lord Jesus Christ, who died for us, that, whether we wake or sleep, we should live together with him." (KJV)

Believers need not fear death or the final judgement. Jesus came and died as our Savior, assuring us of eternal salvation.

(2) The Imminent Return of Jesus Christ – I Thessalonians 1:10; 5:6; James 5:8

> "And to wait for his son from heaven, whom he raised from the dead, even Jesus, which delivered us from the wrath to come." (KJV)

Judgement and wrath lie ahead for the world. Christians have no reason to fear, Jesus, the resurrected one, is coming again to rescue us.

(3) The Work of Jesus Christ – Hebrews 9:12-28

> "Neither by the blood of goats and calves, but by his own blood he entered in once into the holy place, having obtained eternal redemption for us." (KJV)

(a) He entered once; the meaning is that just as the Jewish High Priest entered by the way of the earthly tabernacle, into the Holy of Holies, so Jesus Christ, our great High Priest, has entered in through the tabernacle of the heavens, not made with hands, into the true Holy of Holies above, there to present before God, not with the blood of bulls and goats, but with His own blood, as an expiation for the sins of His people.

(b) Hebrews 10:10-12

"But this man, after He had offered one sacrifice for sins forever, sat down on the right hand of God." (KJV)

This man; Jesus Christ, on the right hand of God; in an exalted state of glory, which is evidence that His atonement once for all is accepted, and is efficacious in securing the salvation of all who believe.

D. The Church During the Tribulation (The Bema Seat Judgement) – I Corinthians 3:11-15; II Corinthians 5:10

"For we must all appear before the Judgement seat of Christ; that everyone may receive the things done in his body, according to that he hath done,whether it be good or bad." (II Cor. 5:10 KJV)

An abiding conviction that each individual will stand at the Judgement-Seat of Christ, and receive according to the deeds done in the body, is adopted to make men circumspect, and lead them most earnestly to desire and diligently to labor that they may be accepted of him.

III. The Tribulation

A. The purpose is to prepare the nation of Israel for her Messiah (Jeremiah 30:7); <u>times of Jacob's trouble</u>; the period of unprecedented difficulty for Israel, as the verse defines, is set in context of Israel's final restoration.

The Church is to be caught out at the beginning of the tribulation, judgement and judged, the Judgement Seat of Christ (II Cor. 5:10). The Jews are to be judged during the tribulation under the Anti-Christ on the earth. Their judgment is known as the "Time of Jacob's Troubles." The Gentiles (nations) are to be judged at the close of the tribulation, when the Lord Jesus Christ shall descend from Heaven and sit on the throne of His glory at Jerusalem.

B. The Chronology of Prophecy – Daniel 9:24-27

(1) Note the weeks are years seventy weeks; that is seventy sabbatical cycles of seven years each for a total of 190 years. The seventy weeks has been decreed. From the destruction of the first temple until the destruction of the second temple; the 70 years of the Babylonians exile plus the 420 years that the second temple stood, bring

an end to sin … and usher in everlasting righteousness. "Seventy weeks" for God to complete the expiation of Israel's sins through affliction, in order to then grant them "everlasting righteousness"; to confirm vision and prophet; to see all the words of the prophets fulfilled; to seal "vision and prophet" – with the building of the second temple.

(2) Compare the time of Matthew 24, and the false peace, as to the rumors of war. – Matthew 24:23-27. Jesus gave seven signs in this passage that would be precursors of His return. The multiple fulfillment theory of biblical prophecy allows these to have dual meaning. Historically, they were signs of the approaching destruction of the temple. Eschatologically, they find ultimate fulfillment in association with Christ's return. Both were part of the question Jesus addressed on this occasion. The signs are: the appearance of false messiahs, the occurrence of wars and rumors of wars, multiple famines, frequent earth quakes, apostasy from the faith, abating love, and worldwide proclamation of the gospel.

> "Then if any man shall say unto you, Lo, here is Christ, or there; believe it not. For there

shall arise false Christs, and
false Prophets, and shall shew
great signs and wonders;
insomuch that, if it were
possible, they shall deceive the
very elect. Behold, I have told
you before, wherefore, if they
shall say unto you, behold, he
is in the desert; go not forth:
behold, he is in the secret
chambers, believe it not. For
as the lightening cometh out
of the east, and shineth even
unto the west; so shall also the
coming of the Son of Man be."
(Matthew 24:23-27 KJV)

C. The Battle of Armageddon, the End of the
Tribulation – Revelation19:17-21)

Armageddon appears to be mainly the place
where the troops will gather together from the
four corners of the earth, and from Armageddon,
the battle will spread out over the entire land of
Palestine.

The destruction of the vicious beast and his host
is symbolized of the destruction of the earthly
powers. The prophet represents false doctrines
of dictatorship under the guise of religion. The
false prophets for a long time succeeded in
deceiving the people and induce them to accept

the mark of the vicious beast and his political power, when the false prophet and his teaching is brought to an end, political corruption, materialism and earthly power will give way to the reign of the Kingdom of God and his Christ. Vicious beasts and false prophets have existed from the very beginning. Their reign will continue until the coming of the reign of Jesus Christ, which according to the scriptures, will be preceded by many great events and signs, war, famine, revolutions, false teachers and false Christs (Matthew 24).

Until all these things are fulfilled, will the reign of justice come? The burning of the vicious beast and false prophet is symbolic of their sudden fall and the end of their power forever. The others will fall with sword are the political and ecclesiastical authorities who had left the truth and were in league with the vicious beast and the prophet. The sword proceeding out of his mouth means that truth will destroy the error. That is, the powers of darkness will be exposed and put to shame.

D. The Prophecy of Isaiah to Israel – Isaiah 40:1-2

Ezra maintains that God punished Israel for her sins twice as severely as He punished the other nations, since He expects more from the Jews (Amos 3:2).

The sufferings of God's people are tied to the purpose and serenity of God. He never forgets His people. They were Babylon's prisoners and His prisoners in Exile. They had paid what they owed plus damages; Exodus 22:1, 7 and 9. God was ready to set them free, even if Babylon was not. No matter how the present appears, God's people can be sure He's working to liberate His people.

The Church is with Christ in Heaven

Rapture

Tribulation	Great Tribulation
3 ½ Years	3 ½ Years

Chapter VII

The Dispensation Of The Kingdom

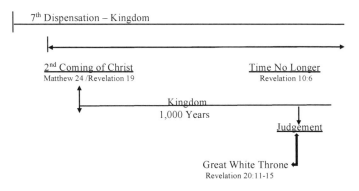

At the end of the seven years of tribulation period, the following events will take place:

(1) The Second Coming of Jesus Christ – (Revelation 19:11-16)

A white horse is symbolical of purity, sincerity and the triumph of truth over evil.

"And out of his mouth goeth a sharp sword, . . ." (Rev. 19:15a KJV)

The sword is symbolical of speech, sharpness and decision. Sharpness is a symbol of prompt decision. The two-edged sword symbolizes justice. Divine justice cannot be perverted, prevented or purchased.

(2) <u>The Battle of Armageddon</u> – Revelation 19:17-21

The angel symbolized the Word of God conveyed to men. "Standing in the Sun" means that the words will be spoken openly and the hidden secrets will be revealed. The sun is a symbol of God, light and truth (verse 17). The reference is to the Battle of Armageddon. The forces of evil will be utterly destroyed. The supper of the great God is symbolical of complete victory over the enemy, whose dead body will be given to the fowls of the air.

(3) <u>The Millennium</u> – 1,000 Years

The Jews, having suffered under many foreign rulers, expected a period of peace and prosperity. This was to be the Messianic Kingdom. The pagan rulers were to be over thrown and God's rule restored. The work of the restoration was extended to the Messiah, who was expected to re-establish the realm of David and gather the scattered people of Israel. Since the destruction of the temple by Titus in A.D. 70, the Jews have dreamed of a third Jewish Common- Wealth.

(4) <u>The First Resurrection of the Consummation of Time</u> – Revelation 20:4-6

Martyrs of the Tribulation - Revelation 20:4

<u>First Resurrection</u>

> "But the rest of the dead live not again until the thousand years were finished, this is the first resurrection." (Rev. 20:5 KJV)

According to the Gospel of Matthew, only one resurrection will take place at the second coming of Christ. The resurrection will be preceded by wars, revolutions, famine, earthquakes and other tribulation. Jesus' coming will be like that of a thief at night. No one will know the day and the hour. After the great signs and tribulations, the sun shall be darkened and the moon shall not give her light, and the whole system heavenly bodies will be destroyed. Then the Son of Man will appear in the clouds of heaven with power and great glory. (Matthew 24:29-31)

According to the Gospels, all men will rise, the good and the bad, but the righteous will receive the reward of everlasting life, while the wicked will rise to receive judgement and punishment.

After the second coming of Jesus Christ, that ends the tribulation period. Seventy-five days will transpire before the Millennium begins. Maybe the judgements will take up the space of the seventy-five days; such as the judgements of the sheep and the goats.

> "When the Son of man shall come in his glory, and all the holy angels with him, then shall he sit upon the throne of his glory: and before him shall be gathered all the nations: and he shall separate them one from another, as a shepherd divideth his sheep from the goats. And he shall set the sheep on his right hand, but the goats on the left." (Matthew 25:31-33 KJV)

The sheep will go into the Millennium Kingdom, and the goats will go into the Lake of Fire.

> "And I saw thrones, and they sat upon them, and judgement was given unto them: and I saw the souls of them that were beheaded for the witness of Jesus, and for the Word of God, and which had not worshipped the beast, neither his image, neither had received his mark upon their foreheads, or in their hands; and they lived and reigned with Christ a thousand years." (Revelation 20:4 KJV)

Thrones, and they sat upon them; representing the exalted and favorite state of the friends of God.

The souls of them; that were put to death for their attachment to Christ.

They lived; best understood figuratively as meaning that they lived in the person, of their successor, as Elijah came and lived in the person of John. (Matthew 4:5; 11:14; 17:1-13)

The men who lived during the thousand years were men of like spirit with those martyrs who suffered for the cause of Jesus, as John was of like spirit of Elijah.

> "And the beast was taken, and with him the false prophets that wroth miracles before him, with which he deceived them that had received the mark of the beast, and them that worshipped his image. These both were cast alive into a lake of fire burning with brim-stone." (Revelation 19:20 KJV)

(a) The Beast (Government Power)
(b) The False Prophet (Anti-Christ)
(c) The Worshippers

Cast into a lake of fire (Revelation 19:20)

<u>Doom of the Remnant-Rulers of the Kingdom</u> – Slain Revelation 19:21

<u>Satan bound for the 1,000 years.</u> – Revelation 20:1-3

The Hebrew prophets, at the outset predicted the destruction of the wicked Gentiles realm and the restoration of Israel through a small remnant. Later, they predicted the destruction of the wicked in general. That is, both the wicked Jews and the Gentiles.

> "Behold, the Lord maketh the earth empty, and maketh it waste, and turneth it upside down, and scattereth abroad the inhabitants thereof. The land shall be utterly emptied, and utterly spoiled: for the Lord hath spoken this word." (Isaiah 24:1,3 KJV)

The destruction is to be followed by the period of restoration and God's rule.

> "And the Lord shall be King over all the earth: in that day shall there be one Lord, and his name one." (Zechariah 14:9 KJV)

Other Prophets also predicted such a period of tribulation to be followed by a bright and hopeful future, a period of peace and prosperity. They shall not hurt nor destroy in all my holy mountain; for the earth shall be full of the knowledge of the Lord, as the waters cover the sea (Isaiah 11:9). The righteous will see the caucuses of the wicked who have transgressed against the Lord (Isaiah 66:24). The angel mentioned here represents God's command at the Battle of Armageddon, resulting in the defeat of the forces of evil and the beginning of the reign of peace. The dragon is the mutual world of deception, ruled by the forces, which from the very beginning have disputed God's authority, and suppressed the truth. The evil will be brought under subjection and ultimate destruction. That is, spiritual understanding and the light of the truth will fill the earth, and darkness will disappear.

The great victory will herald the beginning of the thousand years of peace and tranquility, the Millennium. Living these years, the forces of evil will be inoperative and those who have suffered for the sake of justice will enter into a new life. During these thousand years, God's truth and His authority will be supreme. The Gospel will be preached in all parts of the world for a witness unto all nations. Every individual will have an opportunity to know God and His truth. Nevertheless, some people will reject the word of and rebel against His authority. At the end of the thousand years, Satan is loosed (Revelation 20:3, 7). Satan; though his agents, the beast, the false prophet and those who cooperated with them hath been destroyed, Satan still lived, and if permitted, would tempt men to persecute the Church.

<u>That he should deceive the nations no more;</u> be not permitted to have influence over men, to seduce them into error, tempt them to sin, or solicit them by persecution. He <u>must be loosed;</u> again suffer to tempt men, excite their evil passions, and influence them to array themselves against Christ and His cause.

> "And when the thousand years are expired, Satan shall be loosed out of his prison." (Revelation 20:7 KJV)

The thousand years of peace and tranquility will be once more disturbed by the forces of evil, the righteous will be given a trial. Many men will be misled, but at last, the devil, (the deceiver) and the false prophet will be utterly destroyed. These events will be followed by the final resurrection.

<u>The Last Battle</u> – Revelation 20:8-9

> "And shall go out to deceive the nations which are in the four corners of the earth, Gog and Magog, to gather them together to battle; the number of whom is as the sand of the sea. And they went up on the breath of the earth, and compassed the camp of the saints about, and the beloved city; and fire

came down from God out of heaven, and devoured them." (Revelation 20:8-9 KJV)

He will gather his army from the utmost corners of the world; and even from Gog and Magog, means from China, Japan and Mongolia. These lands were supposed to be the utmost ends of the world. The land of Magog, China, Mongolia and Japan always had a large population – "As the sand of the sea", which means "countless."

Satan Cast into the Lake of Fire – Revelation 20:10

"And the devil that deceived them was cast into the Lake of Fire and Brimstone, where the beast and the false prophet are, and shall be tormented day and night forever and ever." (KJV)

Lake of Fire; hell; the place prepared for the devil and those who cooperate with him in opposing the cause of Christ.

The Second Resurrection or the Last Resurrection – Revelation 20:12-13a

"And I saw the dead, small and great, stand before God; and the books were opened: and another book was opened, which is the Book of Life; and the dead were judged out of those things which were written in the books, according to their works." (KJV)

The books were opened; all the thoughts, feelings and actions of men, as continuity in the book of God's remembrance, were brought to view.

Another book; containing the names, the doings and the sufferings for His sake, of the friends of Christ-called the Lamb's Book of Life.

The Judgement – Revelation 20:13b-15

Verse 13. Death and Hell; the grave and the place of separation, departed spirits. The continuity that the character and conduct of each individual will be laid open at the judgement, and that according to them will be awarded to each the retributions of eternity, should lead us all to so act as we have reasons to believe we shall then, which we have done, and as will, through the grace of God, fit us for the endless joys of heaven.

Verse 14. Death and Hell were cast into the Lake of Fire; here, as in I Corinthians 15:55 – were the words rendered "death" and "grave" are the same as those here rendered "death" and "hell" – death and hell are personified as the enemies and destroyers of men; and such they are utterly abolished. Neither the grave, nor the place of separate spirits shall receive any more victims. (Comparison – Hosea 13:14, "Oh death, I will be Thy plagues; oh grave – the same as hell in the present passage – "I will be Thy destruction", and I Corinthians 15:26, "The last enemy that shall be destroyed is death."

Verse 15. Lake of Fire; the eternal abode of the wicked.

2ⁿᵈ Death – Revelations 20:14 – names absent from the Book of Life.

The Great White Throne Judgement – Revelations 20:11

The Last Judgement Eternal

> "And I saw a great white throne, and Him that sat on it, from whose face the earth and the heaven fled away; and there was found no place for them." (Revelations 20:11 KJV)

The Earth and Heaven Fled Away; expressive of the infinite and over powering Majesty of the Savior when He comes to judgement, the sea gives up the dead, death and hell gives up theirs, and the whole family of man assembles to receive each according to his works. (I Thessalonians 4:16; II Peter 3:10-12) The last judgement will reveal our true righteousness. All our deeds will lay open before God as He judges us.

"He that is unjust, let him be unjust still: and he which is filthy, let him be filthy still: and he that is righteous, let him be righteous still: and he that is holy, let him be holy still." (Revelation 22:11 KJV)

When the end will come, everyone will be caught up as He is. The unjust will be unjust, the filthy will be filthy, and the holy will be holy. That is to say the end will come like a twinkle of the eye. The coming of Jesus Christ will be so sudden, that no one will have a chance to repent. He will come as a thief at night when no one expects Him.

New Heaven and Earth – Revelation 21

Time No Longer – Revelation 10:6

The Seventh Dispensations' Outline

I. The events in the beginning of the Millennium

    A. The term judgement

        1. First Subjects - Revelation 19:20

            (a) Beast; government power
            (b) False Prophet (Anti-Christ)
            (c) The Beast worshippers

        2. Second Subjects – Revelation 19:21

            (a) Doom of the remnant "Kings"

        3. Third Subject – Revelation 20:1-3

            (a) Satan

B. First Resurrection in the Consummation of Time – Revelation 20:4-6

Note: Martyrs of the tribulation- Revelation 20:4

II. The Character of the Millennium

A. Spiritual Character

1. Righteousness – Isaiah 60:21a
2. Truth – Isaiah 60:21b
3. Holiness

(a) The mountain – Psalms 48:1
(b) His house – Ezekiel 43:12

4. Holy Spirit – Joel 2:28-29

B. Some Conditions

1. Peace – Isaiah 2:4; 9:4-7
2. Joy – Isaiah 9:3-4
3. No Sickness – Isaiah 33:24; Genesis 30:17; Ezekiel 34:16

C. The Time of the Millennium – Revelation 20:1-6

D. The Government of the Millennium

   1. Theocracy – Revelation 19:15-16
   2. Messiah the King – Isaiah 2:1-5

E. The Subject of the Millennium

   1. Israel – Jeremiah 31:33-34
   2. Saved Gentile People – Revelation 20:4

III. The Closing Events of the Millennium -

   A. Satan loosed – Revelation 20:30
   B. The last battle – Revelation 20:8-9
   C. Satan cast into the Lake of Fire (Eternal)
   D. The Great White Throne Judgement – Revelation 20:11

      1. The second resurrection (or the last resurrection) – Revelation 20:12-13
      2. The judgement – Revelation 20:13-15

         (a) Second death – Revelation 20:14
         (b) Names absent from the Book of Life – Revelation 20:15

IV. The Last Event

   A. New Heaven and New Earth – Revelation 21:1
   B. New Jerusalem (Holy City) – Revelation 21:2; 21:9-21

C. New Temple – Revelation 21:22
D. New Light – Revelation 21:23-27
E. The People – Revelation 21:3-7
F. The New "Paradise" – Revelation 22:1-17

The New Paradise Outline

I. The New Heaven

    A. The account of – Revelation 21:1
    B. The passing of the present earth

        1. Matthew 24:35
        2. Hebrews 1:10-12

    C. The account of II Peter 3:4-13

        1. The beginning of the earth – II Peter 3:4-5
        2. Judgements on the earth

            (a) Genesis 3:17-18
            (b) II Peter 3:6

        3. The end of the earth – II Peter 3:7-13

II. New Jerusalem

    A. Its origin – Revelation 21:2
    B. Its description – Revelation 9:9-21

1. Note – the size

   (a) City – 12 thousand furlongs square 606 ¾; English feet = 7,261,000 = 1,379 miles square
   (b) Wall – 144 cubits 17.72 inches (common 20.67 inches) long

      Common = 2,551.68 inches - - 212.64 feet; long = 2,976.48 inches - - 248.4 feet

III. The New Temple – Revelation 21:22
IV. The New Light – Revelation 21:23-27
V. The New People – Revelation 21:3-7

   Note: See the description of people that are there – Revelation 21:8

VI. The New Paradise – Revelation 22:1-17

   New heavens and a new earth; Paradise regained; new spiritual environment, new physical conditions, not surrounded by the temptations and defects of this mental life; no more sea. Somethings that use to be have all passed away; death, mourning, curses, tears, sorrow and nights, all have gone. New creative things appear: the River of Life, the Tree of Life, new service, new relationships, new Light, and the new life in the new eternal home. For man, it is a place of rest, joy and an everlasting fellowship with God and His Son Jesus.

Printed in the United States
By Bookmasters